Peg the Red

by Wendy Ellwood

Illustrated by Sophie Holme

Three Little Red Squirrels
Chitter chatter, chitter chatter,
Peg, Ping and Bristle
Nitter natter, nitter natter.

Bristle and Ping race up to the sky

With giant leaps as if they can fly.

Bristle dives down; Ping is hot on his trail.

Ping snatches and catches the tip of his tail.

Now it's Bristle's turn to tag his brother

All watched from below by Mar, our mother.

She loves to see us safe at play,

Darting round the trees in High Hay

Now that the greys have gone away.

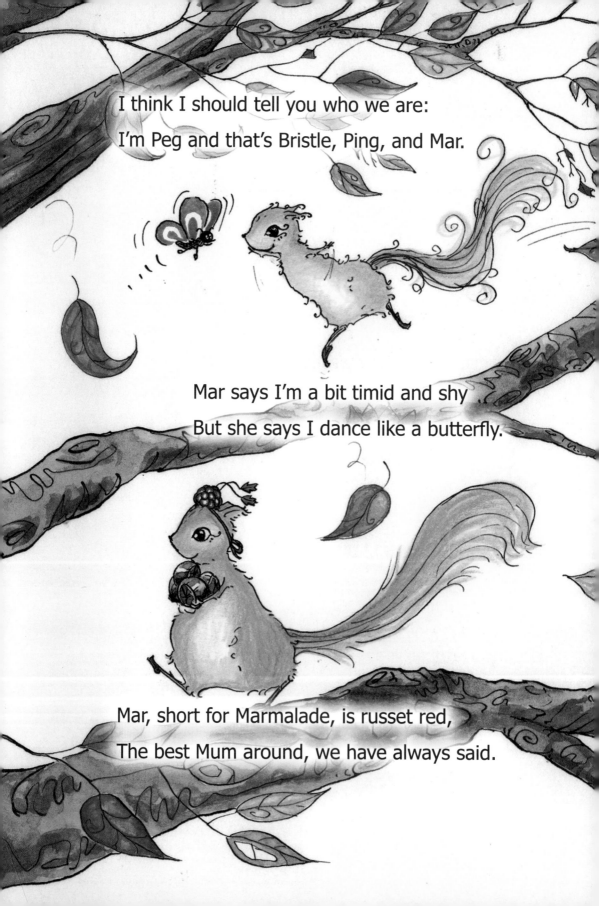

I think I should tell you who we are:
I'm Peg and that's Bristle, Ping, and Mar.

Mar says I'm a bit timid and shy
But she says I dance like a butterfly.

Mar, short for Marmalade, is russet red,
The best Mum around, we have always said.

Bristle's tail is truly amazing
Sweeping behind him, red flames blazing.

With his sharp tufty ears Ping can hear all,
Each chitter, each chatter, no matter how small!

Our Red cousins live in the larch next door.
We forage together for our winter store.

So just to remind you, I am Peg.

Can I tell you about my wobbly leg?

I was dancing, twirling right around,

When I heard an unexpected sound

In the distance, behind a fir tree,

I saw a grey shadow move furtively.

It moved quickly along the ground,

Getting closer with every bound.

It stopped right up in front of my nose;

Fear spread down to the tips of my toes.

"Hi, I'm Nutcase Junior," said the grey.

(I'm the crafty one that got away!)*

Come play by the Lake with me today?"

Mar's warned us not to go with strangers

Behind any tree there could lurk dangers.

She said to ask before we go anywhere;

I think I can see Mar over there.

*
**Did you see
me escape in
Bristle the Red?**

Nutcase J quickly grabbed my arm.

I pulled away in great alarm.

I knew all about the Yankee greys

And their bossy, domineering ways.

I fled nervously through the wood

Running faster than I thought I could.

Out of High Hay, through trees standing tall,

Along a track and over a wall,

Across a field, through a flock of sheep,

Under a gate, to cows half asleep,

Down past a barn, head for the stile.

He's still behind me after many a mile.

Then a mighty roar came from the distance

Which made me fear for my very existence.

ROAR!

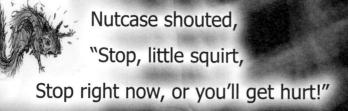

Nutcase shouted,

"Stop, little squirt,

Stop right now, or you'll get hurt!"

I stood in the road, a fearsome place,

Cars whizzing by in front of my face.

Mar warned us about crossing the road,

"Always follow Tufty's safety code." *

But all I could hear were roars and squeals

So instead I darted between the wheels ...

* See Mar's fact file

I lay by the roadside, I couldn't speak,
Out of my mouth came a whimpering squeak.

Back at High Hay I couldn't be found.

They checked through the wood and all around.

They dashed about calling my name

But I was missing. Who was to blame?

Mar called Wainwright Owl to help make a plan.

"Co-ordinate a search, quick as we can.

Send search parties out along each track,

Leave nothing unturned. Just bring Peg back."

In the frosty dark of that winter's night
They were losing hope that I'd be all right.

Then Ping picked up
a distant sound.
He beckoned Mar, his ear to the ground.

Out of High Hay, through trees standing tall,
Along a track and over a wall,
Across a field, through a flock of sheep,
Under a gate, to cows fast asleep,

Down past a barn, head for the stile.

They followed Ping's lead for many a mile.

Then as he heard my whimper close by,

Ping spotted me in the blink of an eye.

They all ran up and hugged me tight
And pranced around in great delight.
I skipped and I tripped and I tried to dance
But with a wobbly leg I had no chance.

There by the roadside, cars whizzing past,
My family around, I felt safe at last.

Mar patched up my sore, injured leg.

"Bristle, can you carry poor, little Peg?"

Safely back home, my story told,

Will a happy ending now unfold?

No, I'm afraid there's more to tell,

We can only hope it turns out well.

Three little red squirrels
Chitter chatter, chitter chatter,
Peg, Ping and Bristle
Nitter natter, nitter natter.
Peg runs from a grey
Pitter patter, pitter patter,
More threats every day
Chitter chatter, chitter chatter.

Part 2

A while after fleeing from Nutcase J

I woke feeling sick one cold winter's day.

My eyes were sticky and I was weepy.

My fur was scabby and I was sleepy.

Cousin Poppi, the Red from next door,

Curled up in a ball, said her eyes were sore.

Cousin Russet stopped racing around;

He lay quite still on the frosty ground.

Mar checked her old medicine store,

Up on her tip toes, tugging the door.

She tried her old cures to make us right.

She bathed our sores, tucked us up tight.

But as each day passed we all got worse.

Was this what they called 'the grey squirrel curse?'

Mar said,

"Ask Wainwright Owl if he knows a cure.

He seems to know things which are quite obscure."

Up the tree Ping and Bristle race.

Down comes Owl, not a second to waste.

"They've all got poxvirus I fear,

The prognosis is not good,I hear.

It's from the Greys who have immunity

It just attacks our Red community.

Queen B Potter makes special concoctions,

I'll ask what she thinks are your best options."

Off flew Owl to find B Potter, The Queen,

She was a recluse and rarely seen.

But with lots of friends on the search

She was soon spotted near Hawkshead Church.

Owl described swelling round eyes and nose,
With nasty sores and scabs between toes.
"Come with me now to Hill Top Farm,
I'll give you some Potter's honey balm."

Along with honey balm she said they would need
To find a rare fungus, a root and a seed.

He took the special balm straight back to Mar,

Mixed with the honey in a green glass jar.

He read the things still to be found

By careful foraging in the ground.

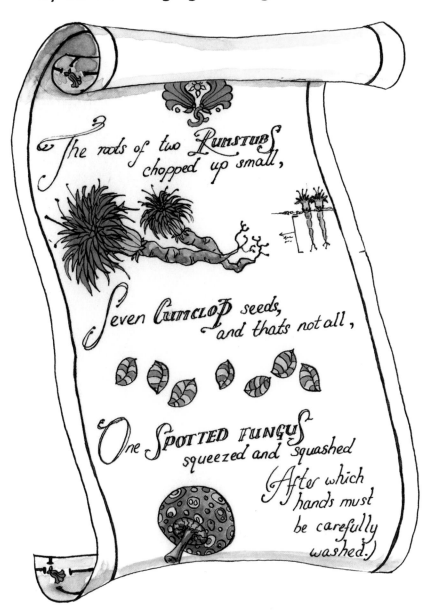

The roots of two RUMSTUBS chopped up small,

Seven CUMCLOD seeds, and thats not all,

One SPOTTED FUNGUS squeezed and squashed (After which hands must be carefully washed.)

Woodland friends helped in the mission

To find a cure for our condition.

Some searched with Bristle out in the field

For cumclop seeds which were well concealed.

Ping and cousins dug beneath tree roots

Frantically looking for rumstub shoots.

As darkness descended on High Hay
They were dirty, tired, in disarray.

Finally Ping found a rumstub weed,

And Bristle raced back with cumclop seeds.

Meantime, on a tree trunk, Mar detected
Spotted fungus to treat the infected.

Into a cauldron went the forest treasures
With B's honey balm, carefully measured.
Mar stirred the mix with a pine wood spoon
While our friends chanted by light of the moon.

Russet, Poppi and I were daubed in the goo,

Dripping and sticky through and through.

Straight back to our beds, not a move did we make.

They began to think we would never wake.

Wainwright heard two Reds had passed away,

Died from the pox after meeting a grey.

My brothers took turns to watch with mother

Till I opened one eye and then the other.

Then Russet woke up and was heard to say,

What am I doing
here in your drey?

Word quickly spread around High Hay,

"Three kittens have kept the pox at bay!"

Mar couldn't believe we were all getting better.

She sat right down and wrote a letter.

Just as we thought we were safe once more
A loud rumbling noise started to roar.

Mar's fact file

Predators, viruses and changes to landscape pose threats to

Red Squirrels:

- Number about 140,000 in the UK, with about 75% of them in Scotland
- Reduced by 95% in the last 50 years. (The introduction of Grey squirrels in the 19th century is the main reason for the decline of the Reds)
- Prefer coniferous forests as they eat cones, shoots, buds, nuts, fungi and berries
- Make dreys out of twigs, moss and leaves in branch forks
- Young are known as kittens. They can live 5 to 6 years in the wild
- Do not hibernate but eat a lot in autumn to stock up for winter
- Are about 20cm long with tail length being 20cm
- Can jump more than 2 metres; can hang upside down; have 4 fingers and 5 toes.

Grey Squirrels:

- Number about 2.5 million in Britain
- Were brought over from North America in the 1870's as ornamental species for the grounds of stately homes
- Are twice the weight of Red Squirrels and they eat seven times more food. They raid Reds' stores of hidden food
- Can eat acorns, unlike Reds, so they survive better where there are oak trees
- Cause damage to trees by stripping the bark
- Breed more frequently and produce more young

Squirrel Poxvirus It is fatal to Reds while Greys are immune to it. Symptoms are skin ulcers, lesions, scabs and lethargy. Reds tend to die in about two weeks. Research carried out at Edinburgh University and by English Nature suggests it 'should be possible to develop a vaccine which would help prevent the decline of the Red Squirrel.'

Scientists from Liverpool University have identified individual Red Squirrels who have contracted but survived the virus.

Lotions and potions and strange sounding notions There are approximately 15,000 types of wild fungi in UK, many are poisonous. Honey has been used for its medicinal properties for over 2,000 years and is still used as a multi-purpose health aid.
Cumclops and Rumstubs have yet to be discovered!

Road kill Over 1 million animals are killed on UK roads every year. Squirrels come to ground when foraging or dispersing. Interventions to reduce road deaths include use of 'Slow Down Squirrel Crossing' signs, or rope bridges, allowing the squirrel to pass over the road without leaving the tree tops. Raising awareness among motorists to reduce speed must be the main aim.

Tufty Fluffytail was born in 1953. Original stories for the Royal Society for the Prevention of Accidents used the squirrel and his friends to teach children basic safety messages Stop! Look! Listen! Tufty Club was established in 1961. At its peak there were 24,500 Tufty clubs. (To view the old TV adverts search YouTube for Tufty the Squirrel).

Beatrix Potter (1886-1943) was born in London. After family holidays in the Lake District she bought Hill Top Farm. She was a keen campaigner on conservation issues. She left all her farms and 4,000 acres of land to the National Trust.

Alfred Wainwright (1907 -1991) His 7 guide books become the standard reference work for Lake District walkers. He wrote 40 other books and guides. Over 2 million copies of his books have been sold.

Hawkshead Church St Michael and All Angels, started as a chapel in 12th century and was extended in 1500. William Wordsworth attended the church regularly between 1778 and 1787 when he lived in Hawkshead and attended the Grammar School.

Where can red squirrels be located?

- Scotland: The Borders, upland forests and lowland woodlands
- England: Poole, Isle of Wight, Formby, Cumbria, Northumberland and Yorkshire
- Wales: Tywi Valley, Anglesey

Website links

www.rsne.org.uk
Red Squirrels Northern England (RSNE)

www.rsst.org.uk
The Red Squirrel Survival Trust is a national body established to ensure the conservation and protection of the red squirrel in the UK.

www.scottishsquirrels.org.uk
Saving Scotland's Red Squirrels is a partnership, led by the Scottish Wildlife

www.cumbriawildlifetrust.org.uk

www.redsquirrels.info
Red squirrel Wales.

For my dear children, Matthew, Alexander and Emma (SH)

For Meg and Heidi, Abbie, Matthew and Finn (WE)

Thanks to Penny

Published in 2016

© Copyright Ellwood & Holme 2016

Illustrations by Sophie Holme
www.blackandwhitedaydreams.com

ISBN: 978-0-9956663-1-3

Book interior and cover layout by Russell Holden
www.pixeltweakspublications.com

Printed by Stramongate Press Ltd, Kendal
www.stramongatepress.co.uk

Colouring Time